S0-DVF-577

PORTLAND

PORTLAND
IMAGE OF A CITY

TEXT BY SPENCER GILL

GRAPHIC ARTS CENTER PUBLISHING COMPANY
PORTLAND, OREGON

International Standard Book Number 0-912856-73-4
Library of Congress Catalog Card Number 81-81320
Copyright© 1981 by Graphic Arts Center Publishing Company
P.O. Box 10306 • Portland, Oregon 97210 • 503/224-7777

Staff for this Book
Editor-in-Charge • Douglas A. Pfeiffer
Text • Spencer Gill
Editing • Norma Catherine Gleason
Design • Robert Reynolds
Typesetter • Paul O. Giesey/Adcrafters
Printer • Graphic Arts Center
Bindery • Lincoln & Allen
Printed in the United States of America

Page ii: Portland is a busy international harbor with the Willamette River providing a fresh-water port deep enough for the
largest ships. Here, a tug and barge pass beneath the Steel
Bridge, 1912 replacement of an earlier double-deck structure
completed in 1888. Page 5: The western approaches and
roadway of the Broadway Bridge (1913) look down on railroad
tracks and depot, once forest-covered land and part of the
Captain John Couch claim of 1845. The first Couch home, a log
cabin, was located near present Union Station which was
constructed in 1890.

Page ii and 5: Photos by John Maddock Roberts.

Opposite: The Coming of the White Man, Washington Park. *Above: Mother and Child* by Hungarian-born, Portland sculptor and teacher Frederick Littman stands on Council Crest. *Below:* Azaleas and magnolias in lovely Crystal Springs Rhododendron Garden. *Overleaf:* East side neighborhoods lie in shadow below highlighted west side.

Opposite and Above, top: Photos by Don Lowe, *Above:* Photo by Ray Atkeson, *Overleaf:* Photo by Robert M. Reynolds.

Portland presents a marriage of many architectural styles. *Opposite:* First Interstate Center is mirrored in windows of Portland Center. *Above:* Recently restored Barber Block on SE Grand Avenue was built near East Portland's 1890 center. *Below:* Bishop's House on SW Stark dates from 1879. *Below, right:* New Market Block once held an elegant theatre. *Overleaf:* Morrison Bridge shimmers in Willamette Center glass.

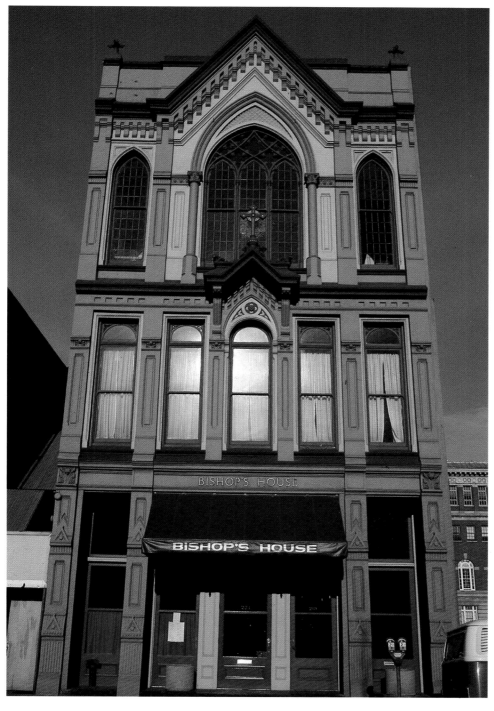

Opposite: Photo by Don Lowe, *Above, top; Above and Overleaf:* Photos by Ron Cronin, *Above, right:* Photo by Kristin Finnegan.

The Japanese Garden, a haven of beauty on the wooded slopes above the Washington Park Rose Gardens. Five traditional Japanese gardens include rocks brought from Mount Hood National Forest and the Columbia River Gorge. *Overleaf: The Dreamer* in Portland Center, a powerful contemporary work by Portland sculptor Manuel Izquierdo.

Opposite: Photo by Paul Victor, *Above, top:* Photo by Edward Gowans, *Above and Overleaf:* Photos by Robert M. Reynolds.

PORTLAND

Portland is a fine summer resort, and many eastern people find the summer coolness of the city by the Willamette as great a contrast from their homes as they desire. The streets are shaded by overarching trees and the high, forest-clad hills that seem to encircle the west side of the city give the stranger a feeling that he is among the mountains...

It has been some seventy-five years since John Gill wrote those words and gave expression to a thought which few, before or since, have voiced in exactly the same way. Yet there is in Portland something of the quality of a resort — a special place in a special setting. The city has grown along the northern plain of the fertile valley where the Willamette River flows to join the waters of the Columbia. The glistening surface of the river, brightly-colored sails, canoes, waterskiers and fishermen suggest attitudes other than work-a-day. As do the tennis courts and swimming pools in parks throughout the city.

Portland lies in a natural amphitheatre of hills green with the varied hues of shrubs and tall trees. From heights of six hundred to one thousand feet, you see the panorama of the great Cascade Range, with its ice-and snow-covered volcanic peaks: lofty Mount Rainier, near Puget Sound; Mount St. Helens, beautiful though no longer perfect; Mount Adams, above the Yakima orchard country; Mount Hood, one of Portland's playgrounds; and Mount Jefferson, more than a hundred miles to the south. Viewed from hills and heights, the city — with its downtown business district, industrial and commercial centers, its homes and parks — becomes a series of patterns on the landscape, linked by the broad ribbon of the river and its bridges.

There are early mornings when Mount Hood rises gleaming white from the shadowed foreground as rosy-fingered dawn touches the sky, clearing away the night. During the day the mountain stands in unrivalled splendor against a background of delicate blue. At dusk, the last rays of sun touch the snowy peak with an apricot glow, an alpenglow, and beyond the west hills the sunset flames orange and cream and cherry red, holding to the last a brilliant line of color until extinguished by the deep purple night.

At other times, storm clouds push in from the southwest, building an ominous blue-black covering over the city while persistent bands of cream-yellow light create momentary scenes of electrifying beauty. And the rains do come. As Samuel Simpson, an Oregon poet born the same year Portland was named, wrote:

> *It is raining, raining, raining!*
> *And my spirit darkly rues*
> *All the pleasures that are waning*
> *In a carnival of blues.*
> *For the constant drone and sputter*
> *Of the shower seems to mutter*
> *Memories of Noah's cruise!*

Portlanders like the rain and miss it when the showers do not come as they should. In the words of an early pioneer: "Let the rains of one long winter percolate down a man's back and he seldom gets away after that. He takes to it, as it were, like the moss on the roof, and becomes a fixture of the location." In fact, Portland enjoys an average annual rainfall of only 37.61 inches, less than Portland, Maine or Boston, Massachusetts which receive more than forty inches of precipitation, not including snow.

An old story quotes a visitor wondering why it rained so much. The reply: "There are so many tall trees the rain clouds can't get by." Still confused, the visitor asks, "Why do the trees grow so tall?" The answer: "It rains so much the trees can't help but grow." The rain, of course, helps sustain the fertile valley, the gardens, lawns, and parks of the city, and the Willamette River and its tributaries. The tall trees, since the city's founding, have helped sustain the lumber and wood products industry.

The first dream of a settlement on the banks of the Willamette near its junction with the Columbia River arose in the feverish imagination of red-headed Boston schoolmaster, Hall J. Kelley. Born in New Hampshire, a graduate of Harvard with a master of arts degree, Kelley taught in public schools, organized a Sunday school, worked for educational reform, and advocated the formation of the Massachusetts Seminary of Arts and Sciences. In the 1820s he became interested in the Oregon Country, first through the journals of Lewis and Clark, then through the stories of returning "Boston Tillicum," as Indians called the American sailing men engaged in fur trade on the Oregon coast.

Kelley's youthful vision took form in 1817 when "the word came expressly to me to go and labor in the field of philanthropic enterprise and promote the propagation of Christianity in the dark and cruel places about the shores of the Pacific." Disseminating propaganda about this rich, undeveloped region, "the most valuable of all unoccupied parts of the earth," in 1829 he founded the American Society for Encouraging the Settlement of the Oregon Country. In 1831 he published *A General Circular to all Persons of*

Portland's first house, Front and Washington Streets. William Overton spent the winter of 1843-1844 here. *Courtesy Oregon Historical Society.*

Good Character who wish to emigrate to the Oregon Territory, priced at 12½ cents.

The circular included a map of his proposed settlement, which lay across the river from "Wappatoo Island," present-day Sauvie Island, on land leading toward the district of St. Johns and Swan Island.

As the self-described "founder and chief pioneer," he received little encouragement and fewer rewards. Boston newspapers referred to him as the "Prophet of Oregon" and to his settlement idea as "Kelley's Folly," and wrote: "We can see no advantage in Oregon which the emigrant may not secure in the state of Maine. The soil is good in both. There are fisheries pertaining to both. If the climate of Oregon is milder, it is not proved that it is better... All that can be done in Oregon within a hundred years is already done in Maine. Above all, she has no Indians to root out with fire and sword, fraudulent treaties or oppressive enactments."

Kelley's writings did arouse the interest of New Englander Nathaniel Wyeth. Wyeth was attracted by the potential riches of trade and organized his own overland expedition in 1832. Wyeth managed to reach Oregon, though his shipment of goods did not. Returning to Cambridge late in 1833, he organized the Columbia River Fishing and Trading Company and outfitted a ship, the *May Dacre,* with goods and supplies. He sent the ship around Cape Horn and led his party overland, both arriving at Fort Vancouver, the Hudson's Bay Company post, late in 1834. Members of his party included Jason and Daniel Lee, Methodist missionaries to the Indians.

Wyeth established a trading post and farm on Wapato Island, but Hudson's Bay Company forced him out of business, and he finally gave up, returning to Boston in 1836. Soon after, the Company put an old trapper, Jean Baptiste Sauvê, in charge of a dairy farm on the island. Meanwhile Kelley had reached the land of his dreams in 1834, but he arrived at Fort Vancouver burning with malarial fever contracted on his trip up from California with a wild band of mountain men, among them Ewing Young and Joseph Gale. Considering them a rough-looking assortment of rogues because of a letter carrying false charges which had preceded their arrival, Dr. John McLoughlin, Chief Factor of the Hudson's Bay Company, refused them entrance. But he did provide medical care and housing for Kelley with a family living outside the stockade. Jason Lee and Wyeth made one call on the invalid, then carefully avoided further meetings with this ailing visionary.

Kelley, who had begun his hegira in 1833, found little congenial on the journey to his paradise. Members of his original expedition robbed and deserted him in St. Louis, and what little remained was taken by authorities in Vera Cruz, Mexico. Making his way to southern California, he met Ewing Young, who was attempting to preserve his furs from Mexican officials. Kelley talked persuasively of the opportunities in the Oregon territory, and thus began the journey of the mountain men and the schoolmaster.

During his period of recovery, Kelley was able to look upon the site of his proposed settlement, although he received threats to his life "if seen on the Wallamet," the name for the river above Willamette Falls. The lower river was known as the Multnomah, after the Indians who had lived on Wapato Island and nearby.

Four years after setting out on his long journey, Kelley was back in Massachusetts. He never returned to Oregon, but for many years continued defending and recounting the history of his dream of a settlement. He died in January, 1874, nearly blind, the seer who prophesized almost five decades earlier that "the time is not far off, when Oregon will be the happy residence of a great and prosperous nation; and will enrich the world with the productions of her soil and labour." His presence in the region is remembered with Kelley Point Park, located at the confluence of the Willamette and Columbia Rivers. Kelley did not lead great throngs through the wilderness to the promised land, but he did persuade an important band of mountain men who helped shape Oregon to journey with him through the "dark and threatening" country.

Originally from the back woods country of Tennessee, Ewing Young opened the Santa Fe Trail, led Kit Carson across the Mojave Desert into California, trapped in the Rockies and the Sierra, and raged at any threat to his reputation or freedom. When Dr. McLoughlin ordered that no one associated with the Company provide him with supplies, he was certain the Doctor wanted to force him out of the country. Defiant and determined, Young, Gale, and fellow rogues stayed and settled in the fertile plains beyond the Tualatin Mountains, west of the Willamette River.

Meanwhile, the Reverends Lee, uncle and nephew, and the two other members of the mission headed down the east side of the Willamette to establish themselves in the valley some ten miles north of present-day Salem. In 1840, Jason Lee and a "great reinforcement" from the east settled around a new mission at Willamette Falls, which was later renamed Oregon City.

Dr. McLoughlin had located his land claim at the Falls in 1829 and set up a community of employees and a sawmill

Henry W. Corbett and Henry Failing homes, 1877-1878, viewed from intersection of S.W. Yamhill and Sixth Avenue. *Courtesy Oregon Historical Society.*

blocks and beyond Third and Washington into cellars as far west as Fifth. Firefighting equipment was put on barges, streets were crossed by planks placed on high trestles, youngsters held canoe and rowboat races, and one lucky mercantile establishment advertised: "It is not necessary to travel on elevated sidewalks to reach our store."

During the 1920s, the old wharves were torn down, and a massive seawall was built along the river, effectively transforming the Willamette into a canal as it passed through the center of the city. But in May, 1948, rivers throughout the Northwest reached flood stage. The Willamette covered Oaks Park, stayed below the sandbagged seawalls, but flooded over the railroad tracks at Union Station. The Columbia, backing up into the Willamette, inundated Sauvie Island farmlands and on May 30 broke through a railroad dike to destroy the homes of more than 18,000 people living at Vanport. Since then, the river has been well-behaved.

For long years, sawmills, industries, ships, and towns dumped their waste, and Portland flushed its sewage into the river. Pollution destroyed the river's salmon, and endangered the health of any who dared venture in, until the city developed sewage disposal and treatment plants in the 1960s, and the Greenway program. Today the river is considered safe enough for swimming thanks to the efforts of conservationists and fishermen. And Portland now has several parks and boat launching sites on the Willamette, including a green mile on the west bank where the city first took root.

During World War I years, yards along the Willamette and Columbia built great numbers of seagoing vessels, but during the 1920s and 30s the ways were comparatively idle. Portland, however, continued to serve, as it does today, as one of the world's great cargo ports. And in the early 1940s, Portland shipbuilding was aroused to action. In the fall of 1941, a century after Gale and his pioneering crew laid the keel of their vessel, the first Liberty ship came down the ways. The ship, launched just a hoop-and-a-holler from Swan Island, was fittingly named the *Star of Oregon.* Among the heros of the war effort, some 40,000 heroines in the Portland area built aircraft carriers, Liberty ships and tankers. Today, the almost daily christening of new ships is a forlorn memory, but under the Port of Portland, Swan Island remains a busy marine center. Its mammoth dry docks form one of the nation's major ship repair facilities including the free world's third largest dry dock.

Before Pettygrove had decided to make his trade with Overton, he surveyed the river in a canoe, taking soundings to make sure that there was year-round deepwater for cargo

ships sailing to Portland. In 1845, Pettygrove built a warehouse and arranged for the building of a wharf at the foot of Washington Street. That same year, Lovejoy sold his interest in the Portland townsite to Benjamin Stark, cargomaster of the *Toulon,* then in harbor. Late in the year, Captain Couch filed his claim on the section just to the north of the Pettygrove-Stark site. And in December, Daniel Lownsdale, a Kentuckian who had spent two years in Europe before coming to Oregon, filed for the square mile to the west.

In 1846, with his wharf up and his wagon road scratched through the Tualatin hills to the valley, Pettygrove moved his family to Portland and opened his second store. Lownsdale's tannery was in business alongside a creek which flowed through what is now the sports field of Multnomah Stadium. James Terwilliger, arrived from New York, was busy in his blacksmith shop next to his house at First and Morrison. Captain Couch announced to shipping friends worldwide that Portland was the head of navigation for ships sailing up the Columbia and the Willamette. John Morrison, a Scot who had learned the carpentry trade in Connecticut, finished Pettygrove's house and went to work on others. And John Waymire, builder of the Pettygrove wharf, constructed a double log cabin which served as warehouse, home, and sometimes a hotel for travelers. His lumber mill, first in Portland, had a long whip-saw, operated, as Scott wrote, "by one man who stood on the log above and did the upstroke, and by another who stood below and did the down stroke and got the dust."

In November, 1846, Captain Nathaniel Crosby once again brought the *Toulon* to Portland and docked at Pettygrove's wharf. He brought with him the news that the boundary question with Great Britain had been settled, and the Oregon Territory was part of the United States. In the following years, the war against the Cayuse Indians and the California Gold Rush contributed to Portland's growth as a supply and shipping center for wheat, flour, lumber and manufactured goods. Gold fever hit many of the men in the territory, among them Terwilliger, who returned with a substantial purse, and Pettygrove, who sold his property to Lownsdale for $5,000 worth of leather, and after a stay in California moved to the shores of the Strait of Juan de Fuca, where he helped build Port Townsend, Washington. Lownsdale subsequently sold half of his half-interest in the townsite to Stephen Coffin from Maine who selected a site at the foot of Jefferson for the city's first steam sawmill, giving impetus to an industry which filled the river with logs and the banks with mills until well into this century.

Portland was not alone in seeking to establish itself on the

Horse-drawn streetcars of the 1880s were replaced by electric trolleys. *Courtesy Oregon Historical Society.*

river. Lot Whitcomb from Vermont founded Milwaukie on the east bank, north of Oregon City, and subsequently brought Swiss engineer Jacob Kamm to build his steamboat and Mississippi River captain John Ainsworth of Ohio to pilot it. Downriver from Portland, Tennessee lawyer Peter Burnett and Kentuckian Morton McCarver built a warehouse and called their harbor settlement Linnton. Across the river, James Johns settled on 640 acres and put up a store. James Stephens, a barrel maker from Virginia, established claim to the east bank, opposite the original clearing, and made plans for the city of East Portland.

During the 1850s, Portland worked to become the river's leading city. Incorporated in 1851, three years later it became the seat of new Multnomah County. Thomas Dryer, printer and newspaperman who came from his native New York by way of San Francisco, was publishing *The Oregonian* each week. The Methodist Church was built, literally, by Reverend James Wilbur, who labored for six days and on the seventh preached. The Congregational Church was erected, and Stephen Coffin deeded ground for the Baptist Church. Trinity Episcopal, First Presbyterian, The Church of the Immaculate Conception, and Congregation Beth Israel were formed.

Public school classes were begun in donated space and within a short time were conducted in their own building, Central School. St. Mary's Academy opened with twelve Sisters from Canada as teachers and six female students, "three Catholic, two Hebrew and one Protestant." W. S. Ladd erected the first of the city's brick buildings. Pioneer Fire Company No. 1 was organized and soon gained its first steam fire engine. Meanwhile, the first water system was pumping water through wooden pipes from Caruthers Creek. Willamette Theatre, with 600 seats, was built and soon presented *Uncle Tom's Cabin, East Lynne,* and *The Drunkard.* The Sons of Temperance numbered Stephen Coffin, Stephen Skidmore, Henry Pittock, and Edward Failing among its abstemious members. A circus came to town, and billiard tables were installed in several saloons.

The 1850s inaugurated the first plank road on the Pacific Coast. Winter rains turned trails into muddy bogs and summer sun hardened wheel tracks into dusty ruts, making rough passage for farmers bringing wheat and produce to the city. A good road became imperative. Hence, the Great Plank Road, built along the southern edge of the townsite, through canyon and across hills. Today a bronze marker on a basalt boulder in the South Park Block adjacent to Jefferson Street commemorates the old road, now Canyon Road, where the loaded farm wagons traveled.

Portland had established its pattern of growth. Although many original buildings are gone, denominations and congregations flourish in this city of churches. St. Mary's Academy continues to provide for its students in a new school on the block west of the old site, while public education includes classes from kindergarten to community college and university. *The Oregonian,* now a daily, maintains its position as the region's leading newspaper, joined by the *Oregon Journal,* and *Willamette Week.*

The fire department, now many companies strong, has a national reputation, and water, no longer drawn from the river or Caruthers Creek, runs from the Bull Run watershed in Mount Hood National Forest to the east. Willamette Theatre has long since disappeared, but many acting groups perform throughout the city, and the Civic Auditorium hosts nationally known touring companies. The last of the old-time saloons is gone, but a number of modern versions invite customers.

City founders also planned an uninterrupted park, some twenty-five blocks long, to the west of the business district, from the river to the north to the hills to the south. Lownsdale's heirs challenged his gift, and Stark broke his pledge, but in 1852, William Chapman gave the blocks extending along Park Avenue between Salmon and Clay.

In recent years, civic-minded Portlanders reclaimed a city block and transformed it into a pleasant, brick-terraced plaza with a fountain, plantings, and places to sit. This popular space, between Washington and Stark along Park Avenue, is named O'Bryant Square in honor of the city's first mayor. In 1869, the area of Captain Couch's holdings on Park between Ankeny and Glisan became the basis of the North Park Blocks — broad, green, tree-lined spaces. The South Park Blocks, where city dandies showed off their horses and rigs, now extend from Salmon to Jackson Street. Today, city police patrol the area on handsome horses.

The promenade is shadowed with great elms, and ornamented with carefully tended lawns and flower beds, fountains, and statues. Bordering the blocks are the solid red-bricked Arlington Club, the massive bronze-doored Masonic Temple, the towered, ivy-adorned First Congregational Church, the quietly elegant Portland Art Museum, the sturdy, wooden-doored St. James Lutheran Church, the monumental Sixth Church of Christ Scientist, the First Christian Church, gleaming with stained glass, and the Oregon Historical Center.

The Oregon Historical Society dates back to 1873, and historically its members have exercised a beneficial influence on the quality of life and the character of the times

Morrison Street at Fifth in 1900. Pioneer Courthouse is partially shown at left; Portland Hotel, at left center, was torn down in the 1950s. *Courtesy Oregon Historical Society.*

during every period. Their motto "to guard the past and foster the future" has inspired superb collections of historical research materials and artifacts and continues to nurture a worthwhile heritage. Since 1900 the Society has published the *Oregon Historical Quarterly,* and, in recent years, books and monographs on the history of the city, state, and region, and their diverse cultural influences. Gallery exhibitions range from the photographs and memorabilia of pioneers and authentically detailed scale models of wagons and stage coaches to the voyages of Captain Cook, the work of contemporary painter Charles Heaney, and the art of Pacific Northwest Indians.

At their southernmost reaches, the blocks enter the campus of Portland State University, which began in the late 1940s as Vanport College. During the 1970s, several streets were closed to cars and the entire space landscaped into a series of terraced esplanades.

In 1871 the city bought forty acres from Amos King, who owned the Lownsdale tannery, and some five hundred acres along hillsides as far east as Eighteenth between Lovejoy and Canyon Road. About City Park, now called Washington Park, Scott wrote that "forty acres is very small for anything really fine. Let six hundred be added to it. A good piece of land along the river, perhaps Ross Island; and a square mile or two on the East side should also be secured before values become too exorbitant." At that time Ross Island was a beautiful wooded expanse frequented by Portlanders who arrived there by canoe and excursion boat for picnics. Since then, sand and gravel companies have torn away at the island so that little is left. Conservationists continue in their efforts to forestall further destruction.

Scott was thankful there was not enough money for the city to take "disastrous steps" to "improve" the forty acres. The decision was "not to dig up the trees but to simply clear away the rubbish and let the native shrubbery and the wild-wood still grow. Little firs, clumps of crooked vine maples, clean-bolled dogwoods, endless bunches of the scarlet flowered currant that flames in the early spring, and many others such as our suns and showers nourish were left in their first estate..."

Today, Portland is hailed nationally for the five thousand park acres on the slopes of the west hills and along the ridges of Tualatin Mountain and for the three thousand additional acres devoted to parks throughout the city. Portland's wealth of parks, within walking distance of almost every neighborhood, are not solely for flowers, trees, and trails, but for baseball, football, and soccer, for classes in arts and crafts, for swimming, tennis, concerts and summer

theatre. Above Canyon Road on the southern slope of Washington Park cluster the Oregon Museum of Science and Industry and Planetarium with natural history and science exhibits. The Forestry Center features a talking tree and working models of sawmill, plywood, and papermaking plants, while the Washington Park Zoo includes an animal park for children, famous Asian elephants, birds, and animals from around the world.

On the hill above the Forestry Center begins the scenic Wildwood Trail which leads through Hoyt Arboretum, linking Washington Park with the parks and sanctuaries of Forest Park. The Arboretum, founded in 1928, has almost eight miles of trails winding through 214 acres forested with over six hundred species of trees, including the world's largest collection of conifers. Identifying markers and guided tours provide a good introduction to a study of arboriculture and silviculture.

To the north, across West Burnside Street, the trail leads up to Pittock Acres Park and the Pittock Mansion, both named for Henry Pittock, who began as a printer for *The Oregonian* in 1853, and with the back salary due him purchased the paper in 1861. Begun in 1909, the mansion, a version of a French Renaissance chateau, required five years to complete. Minutes from downtown, it commands a sweeping panorama of mountains, rivers, and city. In 1964, when a developer planned to dismantle and subdivide the forty-six acre estate, Portlanders initiated a drive for funds and with city and federal help saved the house and grounds. Through the efforts of many volunteers and with assistance from the Oregon Historical Society and the Portland Art Association, the twenty-two-room mansion was restored.

Beyond the landscaped grounds, the twenty-three-mile-long Wildwood Trail continues its meandering way through forests thick with Douglas fir, broadleaf maple, cedar and hemlock, and through sunnier acres, once logged over, where alder and vine maple grow. Curving through areas filled with the varied greens of Oregon grape, salal, elderberry, and fern, the trail opens onto hillside meadows where fire-blackened trunks and giant stumps still show the springboard notches on which oldtime tree fallers stood.

There are more than fifty miles of trails in this remarkable Forest Park, which includes bird sanctuaries managed by the Portland Audubon Society and the deep ravine of Macleay Park. Here tower forest giants growing in 1806, when William Clark saw the hills above the river. And here are trails over which Hudson's Bay Company employees and early settlers drove their cattle and brought their grain from the valley down to the river ports.

The Sunnyside neighborhood, S.E. Thirty-third and Belmont, about 1889-1890. *Courtesy Oregon Historical Society.*

In 1852 Chapman and Lownsdale gave two blocks between Salmon and Madison and Third and Fourth and made possible Portland's earliest park in the original center of downtown. Known as the Plaza Blocks, they have witnessed much of the city's history. Here the arrival of Portland's first intercontinental train was celebrated in 1883, and fifty of the city's pioneers, including Francis Pettygrove, were honored. And here, where elk once grazed, stands the noble and notable statue of an elk, gift in 1900 of David Thompson, mayor from 1879 to 1882. At nineteen, Thompson left his home in Ohio and, driving a band of sheep across the plains, made his way on foot to Oregon City in 1853. The great bronze elk — posed above Main Street traffic — gives a vision of history and place and provides a link with the stalwart men and women who planted themselves firmly in the wilderness and built a city of unique character.

In recent years, the block immediately south, between Madison and Jefferson, was transformed into a plaza and named in honor of Terry Schrunk, mayor from 1957 to 1973. Popular as a lunch and breath-of-fresh-air space for workers from nearby City Hall and the Federal Building, the plaza was the site of festivities when the Trailblazers won the 1977 National Basketball Association championship.

Within the parks lie several remarkable gardens, testimony to a city which has more garden clubs per capita than any other in the nation. Three local clubs planted the seeds or cuttings which grew into the American Rhododendron Society, the American Primrose Society, and the American Rose Society.

In the southeast, not far from the Reed College campus and within putting distance of the Eastmoreland golf course, are the Crystal Springs Rhododendron Gardens, created by the Portland chapter of the Society. In 1950 the Park Bureau gave the land, and Society members provided the rhododendrons, design, and labor for what is now one of the loveliest of city parks. Bridges cross the quiet stream and lake, and youngsters are brought almost year-round to feed ducks, geese, and swans. The more than two thousand native and hybrid rhododendrons are lovingly maintained with the help of Society members.

Almost hidden in glen and glade on the wooded slopes of upper Washington Park is another garden of delight — the Japanese Garden. The Park Bureau provided the happy site, while members of the Japanese Garden Society of Oregon obtained donations to create five traditional gardens. Designed by Professor P. Takuma Tono of Tokyo, there is magic in the way each garden evokes a unique mood and har-

mony: the diminuitive Moss Garden; the controlled Sand Garden with its rock reef standing in a raked sand sea; the Tea Garden with its cottage brought from Japan; the Strolling Pond Garden's pools; the Flat Garden's sculptured shrubs and gourd-shaped islands in a rippled sand lake. Here, in the Japanese Garden, the world is quiet.

A short distance from the Japanese Garden, the Washington Park Rose Gardens open to view. First planned in 1917, the International Rose Test Garden receives new, unnamed roses identified only by number from all over the world. Adjoined by display beds of named roses, these gardens now cover some four acres on terraced slopes looking down on the river and city and out to the mountains of the Cascade Range. From late May until November tens of thousands of blooms blaze. Roses also bloom across the river at Peninsula Park in North Portland. Entry down balustraded brick stairways into the sunken garden brings the visitor to an elegant Victorian bandstand.

Roses were brought to Oregon country by early settlers. A planting made near the mission of Jason Lee flourished, and cuttings provided what became known as the Mission rose. In the 1850s a horticulturist brought stock with him across the country and started a rose nursery in the Tualatin Valley. In 1888, when Mrs. Henry Pittock and friends exhibited roses under a marquee on the grounds of her Washington Street home, Portland had its first rose show. The following year the Trinity Church Guild held the second show and author C.E.S. Wood proposed that a yearly show be held.

In 1904, the president of the Portland Rose Society advocated planting roses along parking strips throughout the city, and in some neighborhoods such plantings are still carefully tended. A few of the once-popular pink Caroline Testout roses remain from hundreds planted just after the turn of the century. In recent years, the city has provided free flowering trees to householders willing to care for them.

In 1905 the Lewis and Clark Exposition held a mammoth rose show to promote Portland's recognition as the "City of Roses." In 1907, the first Rose Festival and Floral Parade, sponsored by the Portland Rose Society, was officially organized. The festive June week now encompasses a variety of stage shows, the rose show, a thematic floral parade, garden judging, and a skiing competition at Mount Hood, all to tell the world that, as expressed by the Mystic Order of the Rose, "a rose for you in Portland grows."

During the 1850s, the foundation of "old money" — a fine social distinction in some circles — was laid. Shipping was on the increase, and gold was discovered in the southern

W. S. Ladd's Hazelfern farm about 1900 is today the Laurelhurst neighborhood. *Courtesy Oregon Historical Society.*

and in the central regions of the state. Population leaped from 820 in 1850 to 2,874 in 1860 and to 8,293 in 1870.

During the 1860s and '70s, Portland continued to emerge from the wilderness, although wild deer still came bounding down Washington Street, and a cougar was shot as it prowled around a kitchen door. Stumps were pulled from the streets, and planks laid as far as Fourth Street and the Plaza. The Unitarian Church was dedicated, the first Orthodox Congregation and The People's Church, now known as the AME Zion Church, were formed. The *Catholic Sentinel* began publication, and Good Samaritan and St. Vincent Hospitals were opened. Plans were made for organizing the YMCA, and the first high school classes were held. Black parents petitioned the school board to gain admission to Central School, and in 1871 Black children were admitted to all schools. The first baseball club played on a field on Oak Street between Fifth and Sixth.

Meanwhile, newspapers reported the successful ascent of Mount Hood by W. S. Powell, George H. Himes, J. S. Newell, Ed W. Cornell, and Simon G. Benson. As many as thirty thousand barrels of salmon were taken from the river in a year, and the first direct shipment of wheat to Europe was made from Portland to Liverpool, England. Skirts with "tilting" hoops came into fashion and created a great demand for ornamental garters. And local brewers, angered at the arrival of a shipload of beer from California, set out barrels of free brew.

The city was establishing its character as one of substance and worth. Thirty-five prominent business and professional men founded the exclusive Social Club, "where they could fraternize for mutual enjoyment and relaxation, and...for discussing their own and Portland's destiny." The newspapers began to refer to the "elite" who were developing a summer colony at Clatsop beaches on the Oregon coast, traveling to the East on business and on pleasure, and sending sons to Ivy League schools. Raising and racing horses became a popular pastime for the well-to-do. As John Ainsworth wrote to a friend, "We have trotting matches with private teams every evening."

Cultural activities were also sponsored. With vocal music its primary interest, the Portland Philharmonic Society was founded, and the elegant New Market Theatre, offering Italian grand opera with full scenery, opened. Soon opera companies, including Signor Bianchi's, were announcing their appearance with "full orchestra and chorus." A Black opera company performed. The Handel and Haydn Musical Society was organized, and both the Amateur Musical Society and the Apollo Club gave their

first concert. In 1895 the Orchestral Union, now the Oregon Symphony Orchestra, was founded.

Today, joined by world-renowned musical artists, the Oregon Symphony Orchestra plays to huge audiences and tours extensively. Famed operatic stars join Portland Opera productions which earn national acclaim for costuming, set design, and musical excellence. The Oregon Repertory Singers and the Portland Symphonic Choir give heralded performances, while jazz, Dixieland, and classical music fill summer parks.

Since its first concert in 1925, the Portland Junior Symphony, now the Portland Youth Philharmonic Orchestra, has received Portland's love and respect. Unique in the nation when it was founded around a nucleus of young people practicing under violin teacher Mary Dodge, the Orchestra has earned an international reputation for its repertoire and performance from audiences in the United States, Europe, and Japan. The long and distinguished history of the Orchestra has been graced by the devoted efforts of enthusiastic and enlightened patrons and board members and by the rare talents of founding conductor Jacques Gershkovitch and composer-conductor Jacob Avshalomov.

There was music, too, in variety halls, saloons, and the parlors of Venus. The settled, church-going, concert-attending town of merchants, bankers, and builders was also the headquarters for a transient population of miners, sailors, lumberjacks, and railroad construction workers. These visitors, passing through on their way to and from gold fields, coastal harbors, foreign ports, and deep woods, sought a less enlightening entertainment of more primal vigor. The leaders of the town supplied the hard goods, and a new group of entrepreneurs provided the hard pleasures.

In 1842 William Johnson, an Englishman who fought valiantly for the Americans on *Old Ironsides* during the War of 1812, planted himself in the woods to the south of future Portland and manufactured "blue ruin," a "vile sort of intoxicating liquor." A few years later the place was a source of whisky which the hardy pioneer would purchase "in moderate quantities returning home on his long, slow journey while he slept by his wagon, often covered by a cloudy sky and exposed to the Oregon mist."

During the 1870s the number of tax-paying saloons approached one hundred, and the Women's Temperance Prayer League began to sing and pray in front of them, daring at times to venture inside and hand out tracts. On one occasion League members were arrested, but the judge dismissed the case. At a subsequent confrontation, the women staged a prayer sit-down and refused to move,

Portland waterfront, north of Steel Bridge, in 1904. *Glass plate photo by A. J. Baker. Courtesy Spencer Gill collection.*

although drenched with water and harassed by saloon patrons. This time the judge convicted them of disorderly conduct and they spent part of a day in jail; the police chief did not think it proper to keep them overnight.

The church women continued their protests against saloons and the "risquê" variety shows whose entertainers mingled with customers to encourage more spending. Visiting preachers denounced the "wicked river city," and local ministers lectured on the evils of drink. When the temples of Bacchus and the chapels of Aphrodite encroached upon shops and churches or vice-versa, moral indignation prompted relocation plans. The dens and denizens of vice moved away from the business district, beyond Stark and across Burnside, to a section called the North End, later known as the Skid Road area.

The bosses of the North End entered politics to protect their business interests, but they had few social associations with the city's moral guardians and "better element." Enterprising daughters of Cupid established temples and friendly relations with leading citizens, who occasionally found themselves barely escaping police raids through unguarded windows. There was also not-so-polite talk about social climbers of low origins and questionable morals becoming members of the upper classes through marriage. One gentleman, chided for taking as wife a lady of dubious background, retorted that he did not want her able to say anything about him that he could not say about her.

The edges of the rough and sometimes violent river town became worn over the years and acquired some measure of smoothness. But one facet has altered little: the frontier attitude of those who "squatted hard" on the land to make it theirs continues strong in those who are "stomping out" a place in the civilized wilderness of today.

One claim to civilization was the 1864 founding of the Library Association. The city's first mayor, Hugh D. O'Bryant, loaned periodicals and books from a shelf in his carpentry shop and opened a reading room in 1850 at Front and Alder. During the 1850s a scattering of subscription libraries and reading rooms opened and closed. In 1863 Leland Wakefield began canvassing for funds for the Library Association and reading room. His first subscriber was William Ladd, and by early 1864 the drive had brought in more than two thousand dollars and five hundred books. The first librarian, Harvey Scott, was 14 when he came overland with his family in 1852. Scott studied law and worked as librarian part-time, until in 1865 he became editor of *The Oregonian.*

First located on the second floor of the Stark Building on Front Street, in 1869 the library moved to larger quarters, provided rent-free in the Ladd and Tilton Bank at the corner of First and Stark. Although there was an initial fee of five dollars and a quarterly dues payment of three dollars, steep figures in those times, membership continued to expand. In 1873, when General Edward Canby was killed during treaty negotiations with the Modoc Indians, Portlanders collected a $5,000 fund for his widow, and Mrs. Canby contributed this money to the Association as well as donating the late General's collection of books.

Over the years there was growing interest in a free library, and in 1891 The Peoples' Free Reading Room and Library Association was established. Located in space near First and West Burnside, it served mainly transients and workers living in the North End. In 1900, its name changed to the Portland Public Library and it moved into space provided on the top floor of City Hall. Toward the end of 1901, an agreement transferred its books to the Library Association, which in March, 1902 became a free public library. Since that time the Association has administered the Multnomah County Library and established reading rooms and book services in communities throughout the area. Funds from Andrew Carnegie helped build branch libraries in East Portland, Sellwood, Albina, and South Portland during 1911 and 1912. In 1913, Central Library, one of Portland's best-loved buildings, was built at SW Tenth and Yamhill.

In 1871 *The Oregonian* urged support for the Library: "This institution has become one of the necessities of Portland, and must be maintained. It has done more to make a favorable impression upon intelligent visitors and sojourners here than any other institution in the city." Today, branch libraries and bookmobiles provide reference books, circulating collections, films, art prints, and musical recordings. The libraries are also busy with story hours and films for children, lectures and films for people of all ages, concerts, and meetings of groups with interests ranging from wild flowers to urban problems. A fine organization, Friends of the Library, encompasses a great cross-section of the populace and provides support with its annual, fund-raising book sale. And if circulation figures are a measure, Portlanders are among the best-read citizens in the nation.

The 1870s brought both destruction and building. Fires in 1873 destroyed more than twenty blocks of buildings from the waterfront to Second Street and Taylor to Clay. Loss was well over a million dollars, and there was almost no insurance. But the seventies also saw the opening of the New Market Theatre with its brilliant gaslight chandeliers, elegant patrons, and grand performances of opera, ballet and

drama. President Grant visited and, at a later date, James L. Sullivan staged a boxing exhibition. With restoration, the building on First between Ankeny and Ash is regaining its former grandeur and life.

During this period, one of Portland's most esteemed buildings opened on the block between Fifth and Sixth, Morrison and Yamhill. Now designated Pioneer Courthouse, headquarters of the Ninth Circuit Court, it was originally the federal post office and subsequently served as the seat of the district court. Admirably restored, the "massive and handsome building" keynotes the downtown, but at its opening it was considered so far from the business district *The Oregonian* suggested a pony express run between the two. At the end of the seventies, Portland businesses began installing a new invention, the telephone. But transmission was sometimes faulty and phones would fail to ring. On many occasions, callers opened their office windows and shouted across the street so that colleagues in other buildings would answer the phone.

During the 1870s and '80s, well-to-do Portlanders traveled to Europe. Stephen Skidmore and James Terwilliger represented Oregon at the great Paris Exposition of 1878. Newspapers reported the comings and goings of the elite and even noted Henry Corbett's purchase of two casks of vintage French wine in Paris for himself and Henry Failing. This period saw Portlanders adorn their elegant mansions with sculpture and paintings from New York and Europe.

There had been little time for art during the early days, although a special 1865 exhibition displayed Albert Bierstadt's painting of Mount Hood. As C. E. S. Wood wrote early in this century: "Our genius is for construction; construction in institutions as well as in stone and mortar....But we are not a people of imagination; not a people of poetry and art, but an unimaginative, plodding, utilitarian and commercial people. ...The dreamer has no place with us, though all which truly lives forever has begun as a dream."

Wood was instrumental, however, in seeing that Stephen Skidmore's dream of a fountain for "horses, men and dogs" be given a form worthy of the city. Colonel Wood called on friend and sculptor Olin Warner to create the fountain. And when the great octagonal granite bowl — complete with watering troughs and bronze Grecian maidens supporting a sculptured bronze basin — was dedicated in 1888, a New York newspaper expressed regret that "sculpture of this high quality" could not be kept in New York. Years of admiration were followed by years of neglect after the city's center shifted away from the fountain's location at First and Ankeny, but the fountain is now restored to its origi-

nal beauty and stands as a reminder of the pride of place held by early Portlanders. Poet Wood composed the inscription gracing the fountain: "Good citizens are the riches of a city."

With the founding of the Portland Art Association in 1892 art took its rightful place. Wealthy patrons established a building fund and donated property for the construction of a museum at Fifth and Taylor which opened in 1905, the first art museum in the Northwest. In 1909 the first classes of the Museum Art School — first professional art school on the West Coast — were held. The Museum and the School, renamed The Pacific Northwest College of Art in 1981, are proof of Portland's "genius for construction in institutions." They also contradict Wood's statement, for they have demonstrated "a people of poetry and art" do live in Portland.

The present building, made possible by the gift of W. B. Ayer, and designed by Portland architect Pietro Belluschi, is itself a work of art. Belluschi, who was responsible for the Solomon and Josephine Hirsch Wing added in the late thirties, also designed the Hoffman Wing housing the College of Art. The subdued statement of the building fits beautifully in its space along the Park Blocks between Jefferson and Madison. The style is modern, yet the rich red-orange brick and the scale are reminiscent of the low brick buildings which once formed a part of Portland's waterfront skyline.

The Museum houses fine collections of European and American art, Northwest Coast Indian art, and African masks. The work of Northwest artists is represented in the permanent collections and is offered in the Museum's rental gallery. Of special interest are the extensive collections of American and European prints and calligraphy dating from the Renaissance. An active Japanese Art Society fosters renewed growth in the museum's excellent Oriental art collection. And the Roberts sculpture collection, established in honor of Portland merchant Evan H. Roberts, offers an impressive range of modern works. Adjacent to the entrance of the College, Madison Avenue was closed and transformed into a handsome mall where sculpture by Richard Serra, Barbara Hepworth, and Conant Meadmore are displayed in a garden setting.

Initially led by Anna B. Crocker and painter Harry F. Wentz, the College of Art continues to inspire students, teachers, and members of the community. Blessed with artists who are also fine teachers, students live and work, as Ms. Crocker once wrote, in an "advancing present...resting firmly upon the past...."

A great and active community of artists and patrons now

The Thompson Elk, in the middle of Main Street between Lownsdale and Chapman Squares, sometime before 1907. *Courtesy Oregon Historical Society.*

enlivens the city, and a number of galleries represent Oregon artists. Lewis and Clark College, Portland State University, and the University of Portland all offer professional art training by well-known, practicing artists. In 1972, through the gifts and efforts of artists and patrons and a grant from the National Endowment for the Arts, the Portland Center for the Visual Arts opened a public gallery. PCVA introduces the work of major contemporary artists inside and outside the Northwest via exhibitions and talks.

Through the enthusiasm and dedicated teaching of the late Lloyd J. Reynolds, Professor of Art at Reed College and instructor at the College of Art, Portland has become a leading center of calligraphy and italic handwriting since the 1940s. Thousands of students of all ages in public and private schools, colleges and universities master the art of written and drawn letter forms. One of the schools offering calligraphy, the Oregon School for Arts and Crafts, began in the home of Julia Hoffman during the same period as the College of Art. Long known for its work in weaving, pottery, and other crafts, the School, first of its kind in the nation, recently moved to handsome new quarters on the west slopes of the Tualatin Hills. The Contemporary Crafts Gallery, opened in 1936 as the Ceramics Studio, also exerts a leadership role in presenting exhibitions which demonstrate the art inherent in the imaginative use of materials.

A number of patrons provided art in public places. The Washington Park statue *The Coming of the White Man* was given in 1905 by the children of David Thompson, while nearby the Indian woman and guide *Sacajawea,* created by Alice Cooper, was presented by Dr. Henry Waldo Coe. Coe also donated the statues of *Theodore Roosevelt* and *Abraham Lincoln* in the Park Blocks, the *Joan of Arc* at NE Thirty-ninth and Glisan, and the *George Washington* at NE Fifty-seventh and Sandy. An immigrant become successful merchant, Joseph Shemanski presented the charming fountain of dryads in the Park Blocks near Salmon. At several locations downtown are the bronze drinking fountains given by lumberman Simon Benson.

In recent years, the city built the Ira M. Keller Fountain, a series of grand cascades and pools forming the forecourt of the Civic Auditorium, and Portland Center's Lovejoy Fountain. And since 1980, Portland has dedicated one percent of construction funds for the purchase of art which will enrich its new buildings. Many contemporary fountains and sculptures enhance the downtown Transit Mall, designed as a promenade and bus corridor on Fifth and Sixth Avenues. Here the city holds its gala *Artquake,* a great summer festival of performances, exhibitions, and demonstrations.

The most significant traveling for the residents of the city commenced during the 1880s and 90s and continued into this century. This was the period when bridges began to span the Willamette and streetcars to reach uptown, downtown and crosstown on both sides of the river, leading to old and new neighborhoods. For Portland is a city of neighborhoods.

As early as the 1850s there had been talk of a bridge across the river to the east side, and in the 1870s a bit of doggerel by Stephen Maybell won popularity: "They're going to build, I feel it yet / A bridge across the Willamette." The first Morrison Bridge, of wood construction, opened in 1887. It remained a toll bridge—five cents for "footmen"—until 1895, when the city bought it and crossings became free. In 1888, the double-deck railroad bridge, the first steel bridge on the West Coast, was completed, and the following year, the upper deck opened for general traffic. Called the Steel Bridge, the name stayed with the present structure which was built in 1912. The first Madison Bridge, also of wood, began accepting toll-payers in the summer of 1891. In November, the city bought it and made it a free bridge. Its replacement, built in 1911, is now known as the Hawthorne Bridge. The first Burnside Bridge, of wrought-iron, was completed in 1894. The present broad span opened in 1926. Broadway Bridge was completed in 1913.

East Portland had grown slowly since James Stephens settled there in 1845. Marshy bogs characterized much of the land close to the river. And as Scott wrote in 1890: "The front is repellent, being largely built over a lowland and gulches. The buildings are yet largely of wood, and the streets are likewise of cheap material, and usually in ill repair." Scott went on to say, however, that "one finds the further streets nicely improved, a large number of cottages and some few handsome houses, good school buildings and a number of home-like churches." East Portland, which had its first horse-drawn streetcar line in 1886, soon saw horse-power replaced by steam-power. The year following the opening of the Morrison Bridge, streetcars traveled from the west side to the east. And as for motor lines, wrote Scott, "this section is gridironed with them."

Much of the area was orchards and small farms, built up mainly by Italian immigrants. During the eighties a number of wholesale and retail produce markets were established, and in time the Italian Ranchers and Growers Association was formed. In 1906, a market building covering the block between SE Third and Union and Main and Madison was built. The Association, the wood structure, and the truck farms are long since gone, as are the once plentiful produce

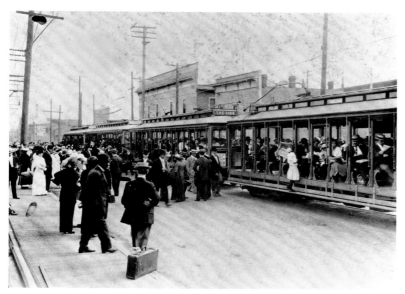

Excursion train to Oaks Amusement Park, 1905 or 1906. The park is still in operation. *Courtesy Oregon Historical Society.*

trucks which traveled through neighborhoods, providing a moveable feast of fresh fruits and vegetables. Some families of Italian descent remain in the produce business, but many more are associated with other businesses and professions, including journalism and the arts.

The first steam-car line traveled as far as the Sunnyside district; later reaching Mount Tabor, a favored district for Scott who had a handsome home there. The Mount, he wrote, "is delightfully still, with an atmosphere at the summit of the most healing and balsamic purity." Some two hundred acres are now a city park, and its six-hundred-foot elevation offers excellent vantage points for viewing the city and surroundings. Mount Tabor is an extinct volcano. For many years its lava and ash were dug out to cover paths in city parks. In 1933, a statue of Harvey Scott by sculptor Gutzon Borglum, who carved the massive presidential heads on Mount Rushmore in South Dakota, was unveiled in the park.

In the late eighties electric trolleys replaced the steam-cars and reached south of East Portland into Brookland, now Brooklyn, "a fine ridge looking down on the deep Willamette and Ross Island" and Sellwood. Sellwood was named for the Reverend John Sellwood, who had bought three hundred acres in the area. Originally, settlers had forced Indians away from their fishing and trading camps along the river in the 1840s, and in 1847, Henderson Luelling took one of the first claims extending from the river. A few years later, his brother Seth, who spelled the family name Lewelling, settled on an adjacent section. Joining together, they set out root stock they had brought across the plains and within a few years had thousands of fruit trees in a great nursery which supplied many Northwest farms and homes. One of their gardeners was a Chinese gentleman called Bing, for whom they named the Bing cherry. Their land now forms part of Sellwood Park.

In the 1880s a real estate company owned mainly by Henry Pittock bought Reverend Sellwood's land and began subdividing it for homesites. Sellwood, which became part of the city in 1893, is a district of modest homes and preserves a strong sense of identity as one of Portland's oldest neighborhoods. A local history group is active as is a branch library, a weekly newspaper, published since 1906, and Antique Row, a street named for its numerous antique shops. The Sellwood Bridge, completed in 1925, arches several blocks north of the site of the old ferry landing. Immediately to the south of Sellwood and the old trolley car barns stands the small neighborhood of Garthwick, where homes face the fairways of Waverly Country Club.

Sellwood flows into Westmoreland, a somewhat newer neighborhood to the east and northeast. A small creek moves slowly through Westmoreland Park, where, in a large casting pool, children race boats they have designed and made from milk cartons. There are also football, soccer, and softball playing fields and a bowling green. To the east lies Eastmoreland, a neighborhood of "gracious living." Developed following the establishment of nearby Reed College, Eastmoreland is graced with tree-lined streets and fine homes ten minutes from downtown.

Interurban trolleys connecting downtown with East Portland, Brooklyn, Sellwood, Milwaukie, Gladstone—once a Chatauqua site — and Oregon City, began in the nineties. One stop, Oaks Amusement Park, built along the river to benefit from visitors to the Lewis and Clark Exposition, continues as a place of pleasure and picnics.

The trolleys branched out to reach other neighborhoods such as Woodstock, Lents, Mount Scott, Montavilla, Richmond, Creston, and Colonial Heights. When East Portland consolidated with Portland in 1891, it included neighborhoods now known as Ladd's Addition and Buckman. To the north was Holladay Addition, which now contains Holladay Park Hospital, new high-rise office buildings, and one of the nation's first great shopping malls, Lloyd Center.

Irvington, to the north of the Center, was named for shipbuilder-sea captain William Irving who in 1852 claimed much of the land on which the district stands. When Irvington became part of Portland in 1891, it lay on the outskirts and its main claim to fame was a racetrack for horses and motorcars in the area of present-day Irving Park. A few mansions were built in the district, and in the years after 1908 it was promoted as an elegant section for the well-to-do. In the 1940s, the district showed signs of deterioration and property prices went down, but in the latter part of the 1960s, younger people began taking up residence, restored and remodeled homes, and built a community spirit centered in great part around the school. Nearby are other substantial neighborhoods: Alameda, Grant Park, extending east to the Hollywood district, and Rose City Park.

Another fine neighborhood which developed about the same time as Irvington is Laurelhurst. The name was given by the promoter who had developed a district of the same name in Seattle. Much of the site was originally William Ladd's Hazelfern farm, which reached from SE Stark to NE Halsey between Twenty-ninth and Forty-fourth. Laurelhurst homes are large, streets are lined with big trees, and the atmosphere is one of comfortable substance. One of the

Sellwood Ferry en route to west bank was in service until the mid-1920s. *Courtesy Oregon Historical Society.*

neighborhood's pleasures is Laurelhurst Park — its large lake, ducks, swans, ancient willow tree, and tall firs. On rare occasions when below-freezing temperatures linger for a week, the lake becomes a temporary ice skating rink, as does Westmoreland's casting pool.

In the summer of 1888, the first electric streetcars began crossing the Steel Bridge, heading from NW Third and Glisan to Williams Avenue, then north into the Albina district. Albina, named by a developer in the 1870s for his wife and daughter, included a sawmill and huge railroad yard, which covered forty blocks fronting the river and provided the main employment. Many German and Irish mechanics moved into the area to take jobs in the rail shops.

Albina was also the main section of the city where Blacks were originally permitted to live, although some lived near the early Chinese district and others rented or owned homes in South Portland. Today, the Albina-Williams Avenue district continues to be the home of many Black people. The riverfront has a number of industries related to ships and railroads as well as grain elevators. On the bluff above stands Emanuel Hospital, an important part of the community and city. Several small city parks dot the neighborhood, including one named for a respected Black physician, Dr. DeNorval Unthank.

In 1889, a steam car began to run from Albina to St. Johns. Between the two districts, and on the North Portland peninsula, the "miniature" trains and trolleys opened up a number of neighborhoods: Overlook, Piedmont, Portsmouth, Kenton, where cattle were driven up the streets to great stockyards, and Mock's Crest and University Park, where the University of Portland is located. In 1901, the Holy Cross Fathers from Notre Dame purchased the campus of the Methodist-Episcopal Portland University, and conducted the school as Columbia University until the 1930s when they changed the name to the University of Portland. If Hall J. Kelley had been successful, the campus might well have been part of his dream settlement. Near the edge of the grounds, overlooking the river, is a marker indicating that in 1806 Clark came upriver as far as the bottomland below.

St. Johns, incorporated as a city in 1865, became part of Portland in 1891, seceded in 1895 because of high taxes and few services, reincorporated in 1903, built its own city hall in 1906, and rejoined Portland in 1915. The handsome, historic city hall, near the east end of the St. Johns Bridge, now serves as police precinct headquarters. Completed in 1931, the magnificent bridge towers more than two hundred feet above the Willamette and its decks give grand vistas up

and down the river. Beneath the bridge a series of great supports soar like graceful gothic arches. Here, citizens created one of the city's special areas: Cathedral Park. Other parks and community centers in this once-remote district include Peninsula and Columbia Parks, Chimney Park and Astronomy Center, and St. Johns. To the north are the Delta Parks and great picnic areas, a public golf course, and the Portland International Raceway.

On the west side, one of the city's oldest neighborhoods is Goose Hollow, located at the base of Portland Heights in an area around SW Eighteenth and Jefferson. Its name, still used, came from the number of geese left to run loose by housewives of the hollow, who engaged in classic donnybrooks about ownership, until a judge divided the flocks evenly and told the women to keep them penned. Slabtown, on the northwest edges of Couch's addition, held great stacks of slabwood — the barked outer cuttings from logs sawn into lumber, which dried in front of homes until the arrival of the traveling sawyer. Cords of wood were seen in other parts of the city as well because wood was the most readily available and cheapest cooking and heating fuel.

At one time, only San Francisco held a Chinatown larger than Portland's. Several thousand Chinese were settled along Second and nearby side streets from Pine to Taylor. Many were brought into the country as cheap labor for railroad construction and land clearing. In Portland, hundreds worked in the salmon canneries, cutting up fish. Some became laundrymen, dishwashers, and houseboys. Others worked at wood-cutting and seasonal agricultural jobs. A small group of families transformed a section in Northwest Portland into farms and supplied householders with fresh vegetables. A few merchants established themselves with retail shops and built import-export businesses. One early observer expressed something of the surface attitude toward this unfamiliar settlement when he wrote: "The wise and inscrutable Celestial will hang out his great diaphanous lanterns with splendid red letters and invite you to his Orient-smelling shop, or serve you chop-suey, delicious tea, almonds and ginger and kumquats..."

During the late eighties an anti-Chinese movement developed all along the West Coast among whites who believed "coolies" were taking their jobs. In Portland sporadic assaults flared, shop windows were broken, and a noisy rally was held in the Plaza. *The Oregonian* denounced the agitation and violence as "rebellion," and city leaders were prepared to use the local militia to prevent destruction. Tong wars within the settlement created violence on occasion, but for the most part the forces of law

Teamsters with wagons on wharf at the foot of S.E. Alder, 1905.
Courtesy Oregon Historical Society.

and order observed a discreet policy of non-intervention.

After 1886, Japanese were permitted legal entry into the country, and during the nineties several hundred settled in Oregon. Many worked farms around Gresham and Hood River, while others established themselves near the Chinese district. Gradually, the Oriental community moved into the North End, where for many years Japanese families owned and operated boardinghouses and small hotels.

There is still a strong sense of community among Portland's Chinese and Japanese, as there is among British, Scandinavian, German, Italian, Irish, Scottish, Jewish, Black, and other pioneer builders. But for many years, with the exception of World War II internment, the members of the Oriental community have not concentrated in any single neighborhood. They reside in all areas and influence the city's entire professional and business life.

The last of the Second Street strongholds was downed some years ago, giving way to a parking lot, and only a few restaurants, stores, clubs, and a language school building around Fourth Street north of Burnside serve as faint reminders of a once great Chinatown. In recent times, the North End area near Burnside, extending from the waterfront to Fourth, has been transformed as buildings restored to their former splendor gain shops, restaurants, and offices. Among the pioneers in the development of Old Town are two brothers of Japanese descent, who also saved one of Portland's oldest department stores and created a multi-storied gallery of shops.

As early as 1892, the first streetcar, a mule-drawn, twelve-passenger discard from San Francisco, began traveling from Glisan to Jefferson on SW First. Within a few years more tracks were laid, horse-drawn cars were acquired, and the line reached from the Union train station, past Chinatown, into South Portland. South Portland was planted on William Johnson's old stomping grounds, later part of the Caruthers and Terwilliger claims. Jewish people from almost every region of the world and Italian immigrants created one of Portland's strongest and most colorful ethnic neighborhoods. Until well into this century, this was the location of two Portland institutions: a bakery which offered delicious cookies, cakes and breads unequaled in the history of rye and wheat, and a delicatessen which offered Italian specialties on one side and Jewish specialties on the other. Great houses mingled with cottages, and the neighborhood was rich in the character of its people. No matter their backgrounds, they shared a vigorous will not only to survive but to succeed. To come from South Portland is a proud badge of honor for those who

grew up there. They shared a special sense of belonging and kinship, as of *landsman* or *compaesano*.

The exodus to other parts of the city had been underway for several years when funds for urban renewal became available. During the 1960s, deteriorating houses and buildings in the section north of the Ross Island Bridge were razed. The Portland Development Commission supervised reconstruction. Now called the Portland Center, the area encompasses new shops and restaurants, office buildings and condominiums, small parks and sculpture, fountains, plazas, and promenades.

To the south of the renewal area is the neighborhood now designated Lair Hill. Named for attorney William Lair Hill, who compiled and published the statutes of Oregon in the late 1880s, the area includes part of his estate as a city park. On the block east stands the historic Neighborhood House erected by the National Council of Jewish Women. Here, in the first settlement house west of the Mississippi, immigrants were offered a variety of classes. Today, the House serves as a center for refugees from southeast Asia.

Not far from the Neighborhood House is an old Orthodox synagogue and a short distance south, the new bee-hive-shaped synagogue of the Sephardic congregation. To the west is the new YMCA Metro Fitness Center and Duniway Park, its jogging track circling an expanse of green playing field. A short walk brings you to the Children's Museum and Lair Hill Art Center. In recent years area residents have restored houses and saved homes from developers' bulldozers by naming Lair Hill a Historic Conservation District.

During the days of horse-drawn streetcars, drivers were sometimes gallant in serving their passengers. On one occasion, the only rider was a young woman who realized after traveling a few blocks north that she was going in the wrong direction. Pulling the bell cord, she told the driver, who stepped down, unhitched the horse, transferred it to the opposite end of the car and turned southward. But by the end of the eighties, horsecars were being replaced by electric trolleys which could reach all areas of the west side. Some neighborhoods, such as Fulton Park, Capitol Hill, and Multnomah, were later served by electric interurban railroads. "Dwellings of wealth and elegance," many still in use, were established on King's Hill above the present Multnomah Stadium. And great houses were going up on Westover, Arlington Heights, and Willamette Heights.

Cable cars led to Portland Heights, but after a few years were replaced by electric trolleys which climbed to Council Crest, the 1851 claim of John Talbot who happened upon the area while searching for a wayward cow. Until the cable

Opposite: O'Bryant Square, on Park Avenue between Stark and Washington Streets, was named for Portland's first mayor, Hugh D. O'Bryant. Dedicated in 1974, the popular downtown plaza was designed by Donald W. Edmundson. *Photo by Robert M. Reynolds.*

car and trolley, Council Crest remained a wild and isolated region. Its name was set in July, 1898 when visitors and Portland hosts to a National Council of Congregational Churches were enjoying a picnic on the hill. Discussion culminated in the modern name, suggested by someone from Portland, Maine. A Talbot daughter said she watched an eruption of Mount St. Helens from Council Crest during the 1850s, and in 1980 many Portlanders came here to watch the mountain in action again.

The surrounding area is now one of Portland's most pleasant residential neighborhoods. To the east, about midway down from the crest, is Marquam Hill and Sam Jackson Park, a gift to the city in 1924 from the C. S. Jackson Family, founders of the *Oregon Journal.* Oregon Health Sciences University, with medical, dental, and nursing schools, as well as the Doernbecher Hospital for Children and the Veterans Hospital is located here.

Along the river side of the hill is Terwilliger Boulevard, one of the city's most scenic ways. From here views look out to downtown, the waterfront, Portland Center, Lair Hill and Corbett areas, the new John's Landing development and across the river to the east side neighborhoods and the Cascade Mountains.

Today, Tri-Met buses serve the city and surrounding Multnomah, Clackamas, and Washington Counties. Gasoline buses were put into service as early as the 1920s on some lines; trackless trolleys began operating in some sections in the late 1930s; the last trolleys were taken off the tracks in 1950. Some Portlanders spent the last day riding the Council Crest, Willamette Heights, and Twenty-Third lines until the cars headed to the barns. Today, all of the diesel buses and passengers from all of the neighborhoods meet one another in downtown Portland's handsomely adorned Transit Mall.

Over the years, the city's economic base has changed with the times and become broader and more diversified. Lumber and shipping continue to be strong factors. The salmon processing and canning industry of early Portland has moved to the coast; the fruit and vegetable canneries are now great processing and freezing plants in Oregon's agricultural lands.

Foundries and manufacturing firms originally producing equipment for the lumber industry have developed new processes and products which meet the needs of material handling and of construction and transportation industries throughout the nation. An oscilliscope designed by a Portlander and Reed College graduate became the basis of an international electronics firm. Additional specialty firms have developed, and there are now several which produce components and elements for the electronics industry.

Companies once making ships' sails, sweaters, gloves, and wool blankets began, long years ago, to manufacture additional products for winter and summer sports and then to create complete style lines which make them leaders in the sportswear and fashion field. In 1888 *The Oregonian* noted: "For a city of its size Portland has more large and successful printing establishments than any other city in the United States." Today, Portland also continues as a major center for quality printing, publishing, and graphic arts.

In 1890 Scott wrote: "While the people of Portland are not mercurial or excitable, and by Californians, or people 'east of the mountains', are even accused of being lymphatic, if not somnolent, they are much given and have been from the earliest times inclined to recreations and public amusements." Portlanders continue in their quiet way to enjoy and protect the pleasures afforded by the special part of the natural world in which they live: Pacific beaches, rivers, lakes and forests, the mountains of the Cascades, and city parks. Portland is not only a "fine summer resort," but also a fine place, spring, fall, and winter. Portlanders may seem "somnolent" to some because their particular conservatism is based upon preserving and maintaining that which they have found good. The city still presents a picture similar to the one described by an English writer who visited in 1877:

Portland seemed to us to be nearly as great a place as San Francisco. The city rises from the water's edge, and covers what used to be pine-clad hills. The depth of water allows the grain-ships to lie alongside the wharves to load, and there is a busy scene with the river steamboats and tugs and ferryboats passing and re-passing. ...We walked through the main streets of the town, and admired the well-filled shops, the broad streets, the houses of the residents, set some little way back from the road, with a little garden to each, filled with flowering-shrubs and flowers. We climbed to the top of the hill behind, and looked over the town to the broad river, with the shipping dotting its surface, the masts and rigging standing out clear in the bright, sunny air; while away, farther to the east, the snowy summit of Mount Hood towered up eleven thousand feet into the sky.

Opposite: A park in the urban renewal area known as Portland Center includes sculpture by Lee Kelly and Bonnie Bronson. *Above:* Playful fountain commissioned for the downtown Transit Mall is a favorite resting spot. *Below:* One of several small Balch Creek waterfalls in Macleay Park. Danford Balch settled in the region in 1850. Merchant Donald Macleay gave the 103-acre site to the city in 1897.

Opposite: Photo by Russell Lamb, *Above, top:* Photo by Kristin Finnegan.

Opposite: Equestrian statue of *Joan of Arc* at NE Thirty-ninth and Glisan was a gift in 1924 from Dr. Henry Waldo Coe, who arranged the casting of the original gilded statue he viewed in Paris. *Below:* The Skidmore Fountain at SW First and Ankeny was designed by Olin Warner and dedicated in 1888, a bequest by druggist Stephen Skidmore for "all that were athirst."

Opposite: Photo by Robert M. Reynolds, *Above:* Photo by Russell Lamb.

Opposite: Elegant cast-iron lights testify for tradition as the Hawthorne Bridge is silhouetted by early morning sun. *Above:* A modern high-rise and the tower of the First Congregational Church (1895). *Below:* A tug passes under Hawthorne Bridge. *Overleaf:* From old South Portland a view of Portland Center, First Interstate Center, and the Georgia-Pacific Building.

Opposite: Photo by Shari Kearney, *Above, top:* Photo by Jeff Becker, *Above:* Photo by Richard Hallwyler, *Overleaf:* Photo by Robert M. Reynolds.

Opposite: Jackson Tower was once headquarters for the *Oregon Journal* C.S. Jackson began publishing in 1902. *Below:* To the left, along SW Taylor, stands the First Baptist Church (1894); to the right stands the Multnomah County Library (1913). *Overleaf:* The city skyline before the sun begins its ascent from behind Mount Hood.

Opposite: Photo by Ron Cronin, *Above:* Photo by Kent Powloski, *Overleaf:* Photo by Becky and Gary Vestal.

Opposite and Below: The Pittock Mansion (1914), now part of the city park system, has been a showplace since the days of owner Henry L. Pittock, a printer who assumed control of *The Oregonian* in 1861.

Opposite: Photo by Robert M. Reynolds, *Above:* Photo by Russell Lamb.

Opposite: Red leaves of a dogwood are part of the fall colors in Washington Park, today a segment of the nearly eight thousand acres of Portland parks. *Below:* A quiet corner of Laurelhurst Park, which contains a lovely lake, tennis courts, playground, and horseshoe pitching area.

Opposite: Photo by by Don Lowe, *Above:* Photo by Lawrence Hudetz.

Opposite: Dawn illuminates downtown skyline and the towers of the Hawthorne Bridge. *Above:* Daffodils and the *Battleship Oregon* Memorial are part of mile-long Waterfront Park, situated on the Willamette's west bank, where the city began in 1845. *Below:* Cathedral Park's name, on the east bank beneath St. Johns Bridge, was inspired by the gothic-style supports.

Opposite: Photo by by Kristin Finnegan, *Above, top:* Photo by Alan Kearney, *Above:* Photo by Ray Atkeson.

Opposite: Agnes Flanagan Chapel, Lewis & Clark College. Founded in 1867, Lewis & Clark includes the Northwestern College of Law. *Above:* Multnomah County Library, designed by Portland architect A.E. Doyle. *Below: Wind Gate,* the work of Portland sculptor Hilda Morris, frames the entry to Eliot Hall, Reed College, also designed by A. E. Doyle.

Opposite: Photo by Ray Atkeson, *Above and Above, top:* Photos by Russell Lamb.

Opposite: Facing City Hall, Terry Schrunk Plaza is a popular meeting place for lunching alfresco, reading, or espousing causes. *Above:* Fruit and vegetable stand. *Below:* Gentle rains and cloudy days are brightened by vivid umbrellas. *Bottom:* Spring flowers announce a new season at the Lloyd Center Mall. *Overleaf:* Gigantic cranes at Swan Island repair yards.

Opposite: Photo by M. Misha Creditor, *Above, top:* Photo by Todd McClelland/Odyssey Productions, Inc., *Above:* Photo by Tim Jewett, *Below:* Photo by Ancil Nance, *Overleaf:* Photo by Jeff Becker.

Ships have entered Portland's harbor in ever-increasing number and size since the 1840s. *Opposite:* Boatswain's chair provides a high seat for close inspection and work. *Above:* Propellers indicate size of harbor vessels. *Below:* Mammoth dry docks at Swan Island serve as a major ship repair facility. *Below, side:* Aerial view is of a tanker in channel near Swan Island. *Overleaf:* Interstate 5 parallels Willamette's east bank.

Opposite: Photo by Richard Hallwyler, *Above, top, Above, right, Above:* Photo by Port of Portland/Jim Douglas, *Overleaf:* Photo by Alan Kearney.

Opposite and Below: The Transit Mall brings a new look to downtown. Fifth and Sixth Avenues are transformed into unique bus corridors with red brick paving, landscaped walkways, fountains, and sculpture. Color-coded maps, closed-circuit television, animal and floral symbols, and modern buses serve passengers.

Opposite: Photo by Kristin Finnegan, *Above:* Photo by Russell Lamb.

Portland, the City of Roses, is also known as the City of Lights. *Opposite:* The moon hovers above the east side. *Above:* The sun emerges from behind Mount Hood. *Below:* Memorial Coliseum seats more than 13,000, hosts conventions, trade shows, concerts, and sports events.

Opposite: Photo by Becky and Gary Vestal, *Above, top:* Photo by Russ Keller, *Above:* Photo by Ray Atkeson.

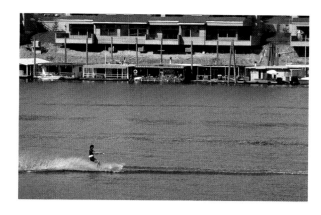

Since cargo vessels moved under wind and canoes were paddled on romantic excursions, the Willamette has been a river for work and play. *Opposite:* Sailing is almost a year-round activity. *Above:* Water-skier glides past houseboats on the west bank. *Below:* Sailboats moored at a marina.

Opposite: Photo by Photo Art, *Above, top:* Photo by Kristin Finnegan, *Above:* Photo by Russell Lamb.

The Plaza Blocks, between Salmon and Madison and SW Third and Fourth, were gifts in 1852 from pioneers William Chapman and Daniel Lownsdale. *Opposite:* In Chapman Square, descendants of ancient Chinese gingko trees create a golden canopy. *Below:* Checker players enjoy the amenities of Lownsdale Square.

Opposite: Photo by Alan Kearney, *Above:* Photo by Don Lowe.

Opposite: Joggers enjoy changing vistas of city as they run along path adjacent to Terwilliger Boulevard. *Above:* Historic sycamore at corner of SW Main and Park was planted a century ago. *Below:* Rare snowfall decorates statue of *Theodore Roosevelt* in the South Park Block between Portland Art Museum and Oregon Historical Center. *Overleaf:* The Portland International Airport is silhouetted against the setting sun.

Opposite: Photo by Ancil Nance, *Above, top:* Photo by Kent Powloski, *Above:* Photo by Ron Cronin, *Overleaf:* Photo by Jeff Becker.

Opposite: Stained glass window glows in All Saints Catholic Church at NE Thirty-ninth and Glisan. Above: Temple Beth Israel, designed by Portland architects Herman Brookman and Morris Whitehouse in 1926. Below: Portland Center and Church of St. Michael the Archangel, which has served parishioners since 1901. Below, side: Monastery and gardens of the Servite Fathers. Overleaf: The Fremont Bridge.

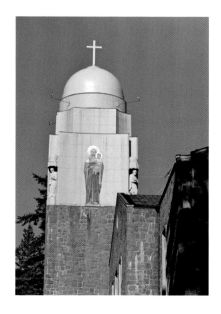

Opposite: Photo by Darlene Dehlin, Above, top and Above: Photos by Robert M. Reynolds, Above, left: Photo by D. Deane Ingram, Overleaf: Photo by Ancil Nance.

Opposite: Ira M. Keller Memorial Fountain at SW Third between Columbia and Clay. Thirteen thousand gallons of water per minute cascade into streams and pools designed in 1969 by Lawrence Halprin and Angela Danadjieva. *Above:* Civic Auditorium hosts concerts, opera, Broadway shows. *Below:* South Park Block elms and First Congregational Church tower.

Opposite: Photo by D. Deane Ingram, *Above, top:* Photo by Port of Portland/Jim Douglas, *Above:* Photo by Russell Lamb.

The Rose Festival, held every June since 1906, includes the crowning of the Queen, a grand floral parade, a bicycle race, ski competition, stage shows, and carnival. *Opposite:* Antique cars bedecked with flowers join Rose Festival parade. *Above:* Swinging chair ride, Rose Festival Fun Center, Waterfront Park. *Below:* Swirling lights pattern waterfront where U.S. Navy ships are moored.

Opposite: Photo by Kristin Finnegan, *Above, top:* Photo by R. Dennis Wiancko, *Above:* Photo by D. Deane Ingram.

Opposite: Fireboats put on a water display during Rose Festival; in the background, the carnival center in Waterfront Park. *Above:* Navy ship and escort with Fremont, Broadway, and Steel bridges in distance. *Below:* Flower-decorated horses join Rose Festival parade.

Opposite and Above, top: Photo by Ancil Nance, *Above, right:* Photo by Russell Lamb, *Above:* Photo by Kristin Finnegan.

Opposite: Firefighters quench blaze in the Blagen Block, now handsomely restored. *Above:* Parking patrol deputy drinks from one of lumberman Simon Benson's fountains. An immigrant, Benson built a famous hotel and gave $100,000 for a technical school. *Below:* Portland's finest ride patrol in parks. Police maintain a museum in Old Town, where photographs, uniforms, equipment, and stories bring history to life.

Opposite: **Photo by Photo Art,** *Above, top:* Photo by by **Becky** and **Gary Vestal,** *Above:* Photo by Russell Lamb.

Opposite: Tugs now towing sand, gravel, and equipment once pulled huge rafts of logs. *Above:* During salmon runs, passing tugs sound warnings to sports fishermen. *Below:* A fireboat patrols Willamette near Morrison Bridge. *Overleaf:* Steam and ash plume moves east during July 22, 1980 eruption of Mount St. Helens. Most violent eruption occurred May 18, 1980.

Opposite and Above, top: Photos by Jim Douglas, *Above:* Photo by Don Lowe, *Overleaf:* Photo by Ray Atkeson.

Opposite: Mount Hood, fifty miles east of Portland, 11,235 feet high, offers downhill slopes and cross-country trails through evergreen forests and mountain meadows near alpine lakes. *Above:* Columbia River Gorge offers scenic vistas. *Below:* One hundred miles west, sandy beaches, rocky headlands, campgrounds, and great resort areas spell the Oregon Coast. *Overleaf:* Rose Cup race attracts a great field of starters.

Opposite: Photo by Photo Art, *Above, top and Above:* Photos by Russell Lamb, *Overleaf:* Photo by Don Lowe.

Opposite: Geodesic dome of the Planetarium stands at entrance to Oregon Museum of Science and Industry, an educational center with displays and films including a walk-in heart and ship's bridge. *Below:* The Western Forestry Center includes a talking tree and a working model of a sawmill and papermaking plant. Nearby, Hoyt Arboretum holds eight miles of trails and over 650 species of trees.

Opposite: Photo by Anne Hinds, *Above:* Photo by Ray Atkeson.

The Washington Park Zoo began with the birds and bears of Richard Knight, a sailor turned druggist. The Zoo is noted for the variety of its animals, the Children's Zoo, and the Washington Park & Zoo Railway which travels through Zoo grounds to scenic views, the International Rose Test Gardens, and Japanese Garden. *Opposite:* Me-Tu, half sister to the famous Packy, was born at the Zoo in 1964.

Opposite; Above, top and Above: Photos by Becky and Gary Vestal, *Below:* Photo by Kristin Finnegan.

Opposite: Stairs lead to the heights above SW Broadway. *Above:* Jogger works out at Duniway Park whose name honors Abigail Scott Duniway, writer, publisher, and leader in the women's suffrage movement. *Below:* Ferns, vine maple, and Douglas fir trees in Macleay Park are typical of many sections in the city's parks along the west hills.

Opposite and Above, top: Photos by Dave Davidson, *Above:* Photo by Lawrence Hudetz.

ERECTED
BY
THE
CITIZENS
OF
OREGON
TO
THE
DEAD
OF
THE
SECOND
OREGON
UNITED
STATES
VOLUNTEER
INFANTRY

Opposite: 1904 Soldiers' Monument in Lownsdale Square is dedicated to the dead of the Second Oregon Volunteer Infantry of the Spanish-American War. *Below:* Contemporary steel and porcelain enamel sculpture, the work of John Killmaster, is located at SW Main and Sixth Avenue on the Transit Mall.

Opposite and Above: Photos by Russell Lamb.

Opposite: Fiery furnace in steel foundry produces specialized castings and equipment for industries and firms throughout the world. *Below:* Oil refinery in northwest industrial area indicates broad economic base of the city, which includes forest products, electronics, chemicals, and famous-label clothing. *Overleaf:* Sailing, a popular recreational activity.

Opposite: Photo by Michael Lloyd, *Overleaf:* Photo by John Maher.

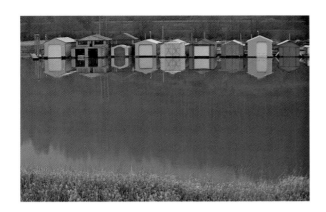

Opposite: Building continues as a major force in city growth. *Above:* Houseboats on tranquil channel near Sauvie Island. *Below:* An aerial view from the northeast includes Memorial Coliseum, square building at left center; downtown at upper right, and Portland's numerous bridges. *Overleaf:* Contemporary office building creates geometric forms.

Opposite: Photo by M. Misha Creditor, *Above, top and Overleaf:* Photos by Kristin Finnegan, *Above:* Photo by Russell Lamb.

Opposite: Portland's liquid sunshine highlights brick patterns of downtown Transit Mall. Above: Buses come and go continually. Passengers wait, but not for long. Below: Marble pillars support rotunda at east entry of City Hall, erected in 1895 to a design by Portland architects Whidden and Lewis.

Opposite: Photo by Kristin Finnegan, Above, top: Photo by Michael Lloyd, Above: Photo by Russell Lamb.

Opposite: Ice on the river is a rare sight. In the 1920s, newspapers said a daring young man walked across the frozen Willamette. *Above:* Painted white fences popularly adorned and defined the homestead. Today, natural cedar encloses patios and garden areas. *Below:* Plantings of rhododendrons and azaleas are seen in almost every part of the city.

Opposite: Photo by Russell Lamb, *Above, top:* Photo by R. Dennis Wiancko, *Above:* Photo by Ray Atkeson.

113

Opposite: Artquake transforms Transit Mall with galleries, crafts, theatre, dance, poetry, music, and ethnic foods. *Above:* Member of Portland Youth Philharmonic Orchestra symbolizes city interest in performing arts. *Below:* Washington Park Amphitheatre hosts operas, concerts, dance, and theatre. *Bottom:* Early morning workout at Portland Meadows track.

Opposite: Photo by Don Lowe, *Above, top:* Photo by Odyssey Productions, *Above:* Photo by D. Deane Ingram, *Below:* Photo by Anne Hinds.

Opposite: Portland State University offers programs to 15,000 students. *Above:* The Oregon Historical Center holds in trust a rich heritage with its museum, library, press, and bookstore. *Below: Windship* by Keith Jellum at The Oregon School for Arts and Crafts. *Bottom:* The Portland Art Museum, designed by Pietro Belluschi, includes galleries, the Northwest Film Study Center, and the Pacific Northwest College of Art.

Opposite and Above, top: Photos by Robert M. Reynolds, *Above:* Photo by Keith Rowell, *Below:* Photo by Photo Art.

Opposite: The Marquam Bridge, part of Interstate 5, carries traffic across the Willamette. *Above:* Portland streets display fine examples of foundry workers' art. *Below:* Portlanders enjoy walking in the rain. *Overleaf:* On the east side, great forests became farms and orchards, then, with time farms and orchards became neighborhoods and business centers.

Opposite: Photo by Kristin Finnegan, *Above, top:* Photo by Kent Powloski, *Above:* Photo by Michael Lloyd, *Overleaf:* Photo by Alan Kearney.

Opposite: West side riverfront skyline. *Above:* One of the delights of living in Portland: Crystal Springs Rhododendron Garden. *Below:* Winter-morning fog blankets the city below Portland Heights. Peak in distance is Mount Adams in Washington's Yakima orchard region. *Overleaf:* Washington Park provides wonderful vistas of the city and Mount Hood.

Opposite: Photo by Russell Lamb, *Above, top:* Photo by Michael Lloyd, *Above:* Photo by Ray Atkeson, *Overleaf:* Photo by Russ Keller.

Opposite: In the words of the members of the Mystic Order of the Rose, "For you a rose in Portland grows." *Below:* This lovely corner of Washington Park is typical of many parks throughout the city, and contains rhododendrons, camellias, azaleas, and lilac as well as tennis courts and picnic areas.

Opposite: Photo by Becky and Gary Vestal, *Above:* Photo by Tim Jewett.

The Port of Portland Paddlewheeler about to Pass under the
Fremont Bridge over the Willamette River
in Portland, Oregon.